PAPER SNOWFLAKE

For All Ages

by Robert P. Kelley

Just Write Publishing Co.
2577 Butte Circle • Sedalia, CO 80135
303-688-4704

Published in the United States of America.
All rights reserved under the Pan American and International Copyright Conventions
Copyright © 1996 by Robert P. Kelley
Papersnowflakes for all ages is a new work first published in 1996.

10 9 8 7 6 5 4 3 2 1

- ✂ - -

ORDER FORM – *Makes a great gift!*

Ordered by

Name _____

Address _____

City _____ State _____ Zip _____

Phone # _____ - _____ - _____

Ship to *(if different than ordered by)*

Name _____

Address _____

City _____ State _____ Zip _____

Phone # _____ - _____ - _____

Paper Snowflakes for all ages
Workbook
ISBN# 0-9636818-4-2 • $9.95 + $2.05 each
shipping and handling • 112 pages, 55 designs

Paper Snowflakes for all ages
Hard Cover ~ for photocopying only.
ISBN# 0-9636818-3-4 • $19.95 + $3.05 each
shipping and handling • 128 pages, <u>120 designs</u> !

Shouldn't your library have one?

Send to:

Just Write Publishing Co.
2577 Butte Circle • Sedalia, CO 80135
303-688-4704

# of Books	Total
	$
	$
Colorado residents add 3% Sales Tax	$
TOTAL AMOUNT ENCLOSED	$

❃ *Thank you for your order* ❃ *Please allow 2 to 4 weeks for delivery* ❃

Crystal Plate
With Simple Extensions

Hold design as shown and fold, then cut out black areas

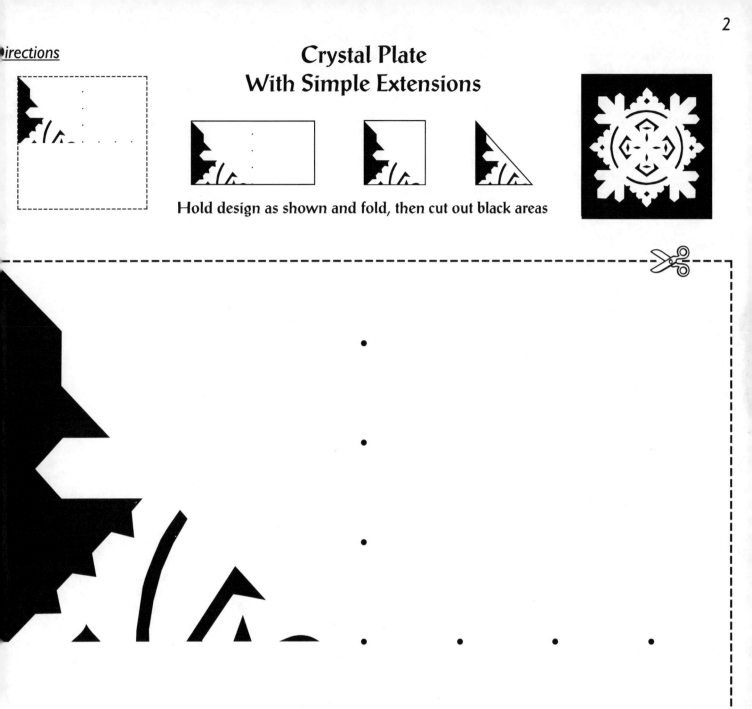

Snowflake Doily

Directions

Hold design as shown and fold, then cut out black areas

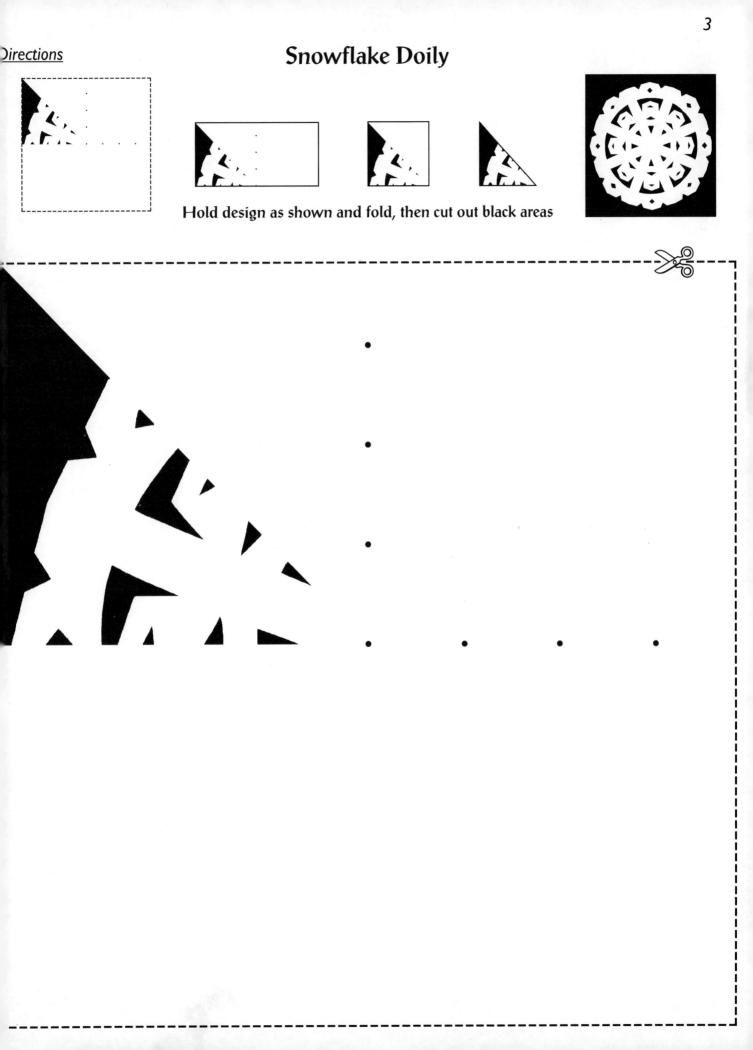

Broad Branch Crystal

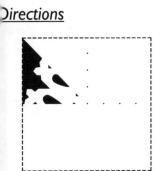    

Hold design as shown and fold, then cut out black areas

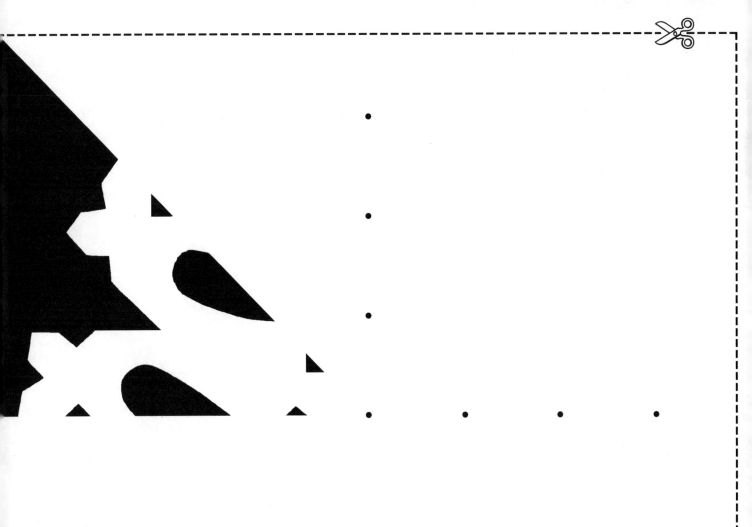

Broad Branch Crystal

Directions

Hold design as shown and fold, then cut out black areas

Directions

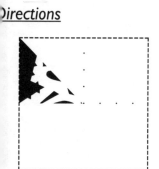

Mom's Snowflake

Hold design as shown and fold, then cut out black areas

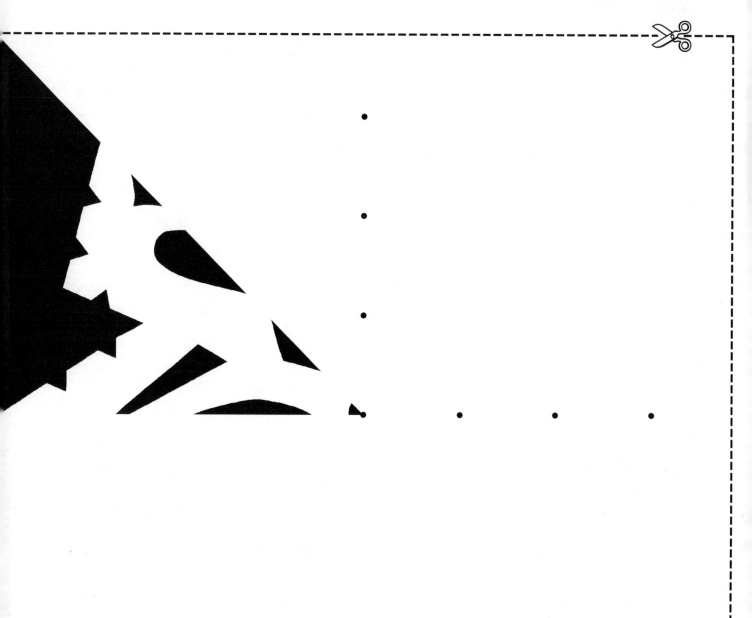

Broad Branch Crystal

Hold design as shown and fold, then cut out black areas

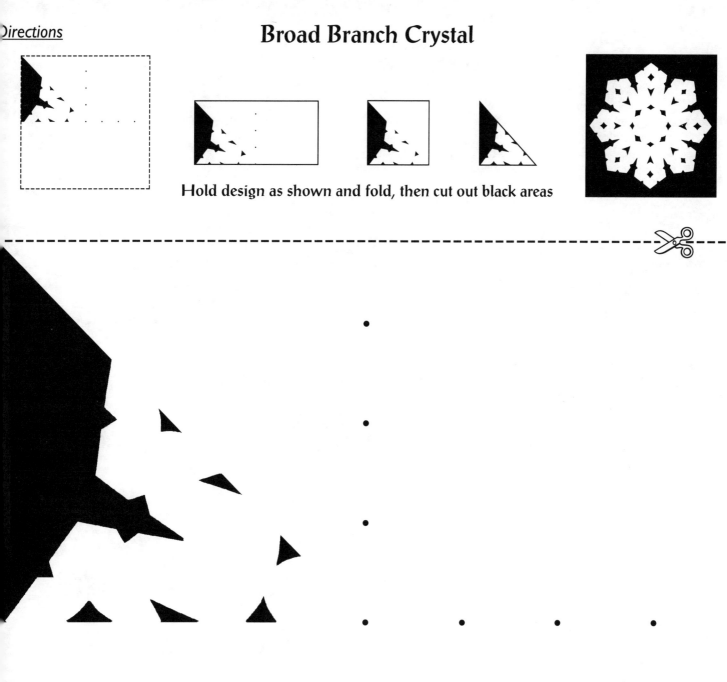

Plate and Broad Branch Crystal

Hold design as shown and fold, then cut out black areas

Crystal With Sector Branches

irections

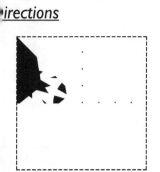

Hold design as shown and fold, then cut out black areas

Directions

Stellar Star Crystal

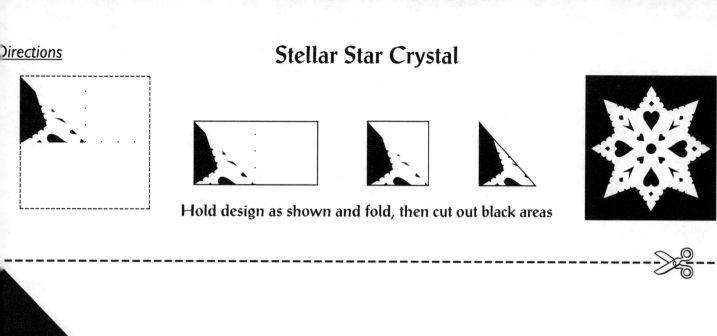

Hold design as shown and fold, then cut out black areas

Broad Branch Crystal

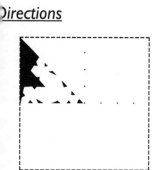

Hold design as shown and fold, then cut out black areas

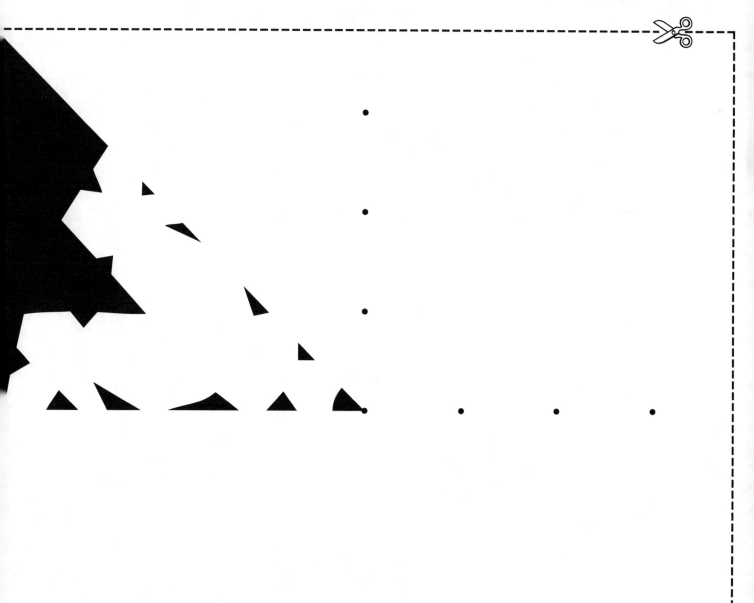

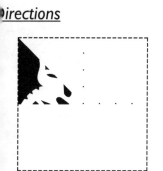 Directions

Valentine Snowflake

Hold design as shown and fold, then cut out black areas

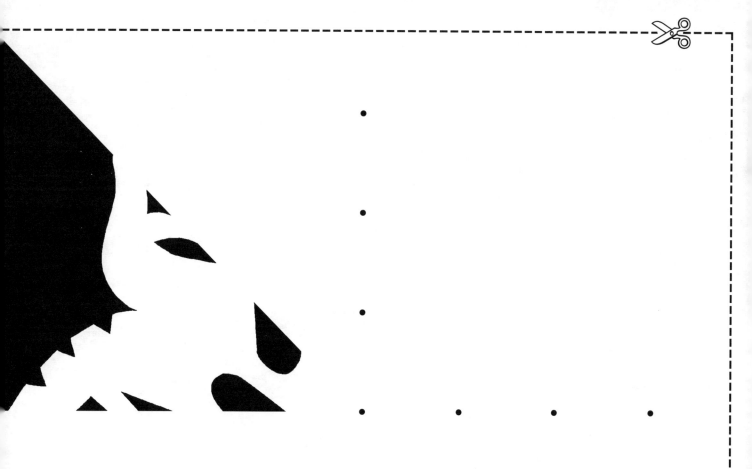

Snowflake Doily

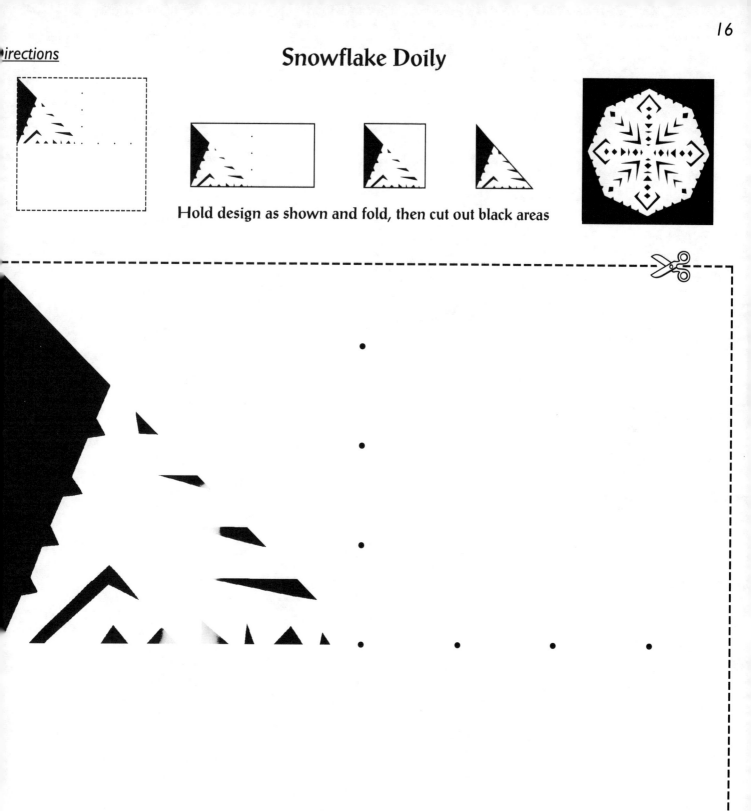

Hold design as shown and fold, then cut out black areas

Directions

Stellar Crystal
With Plate Ends

Hold design as shown and fold, then cut out black areas

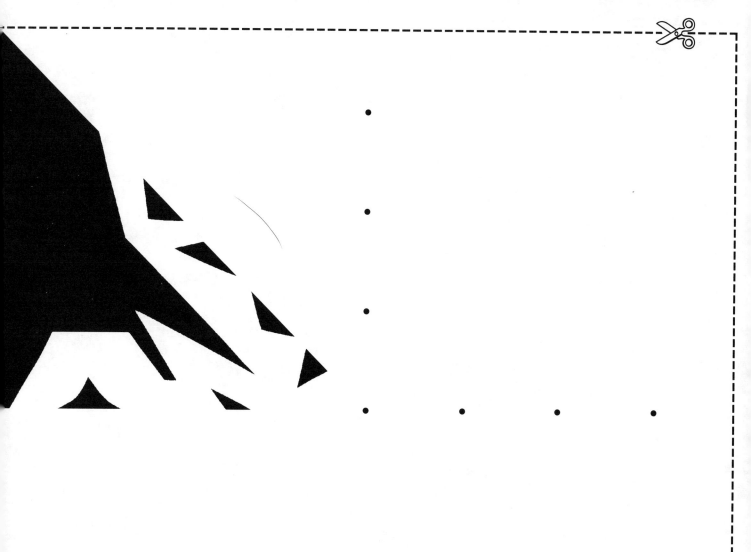

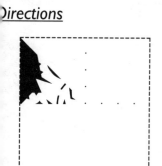

Fred The Snowflake

Hold design as shown and fold, then cut out black areas

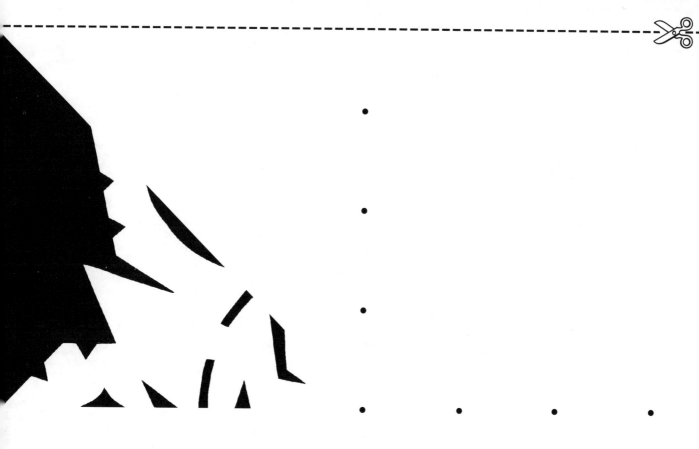

Broad Branch Crystal

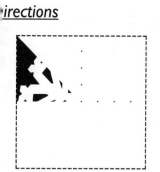

Hold design as shown and fold, then cut out black areas

Crystal Plate With Simple Extensions

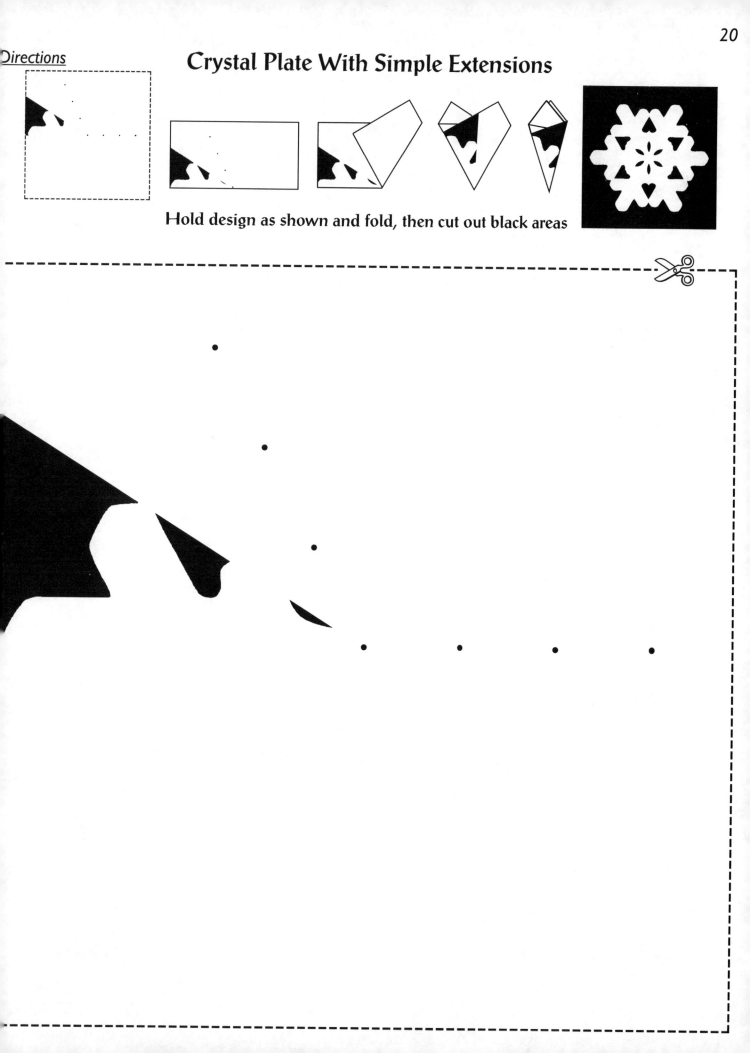

Hold design as shown and fold, then cut out black areas

Directions

Dendritic Crystal With Plate Ends

Hold design as shown and fold, then cut out black areas

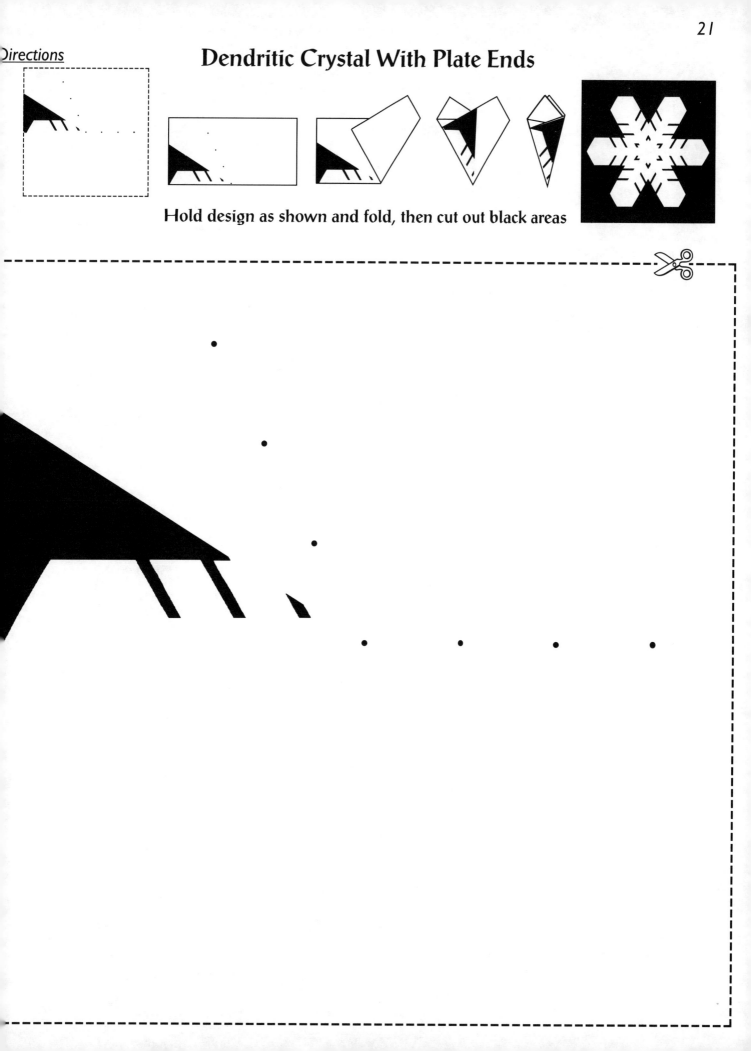

Broad Branch Crystal

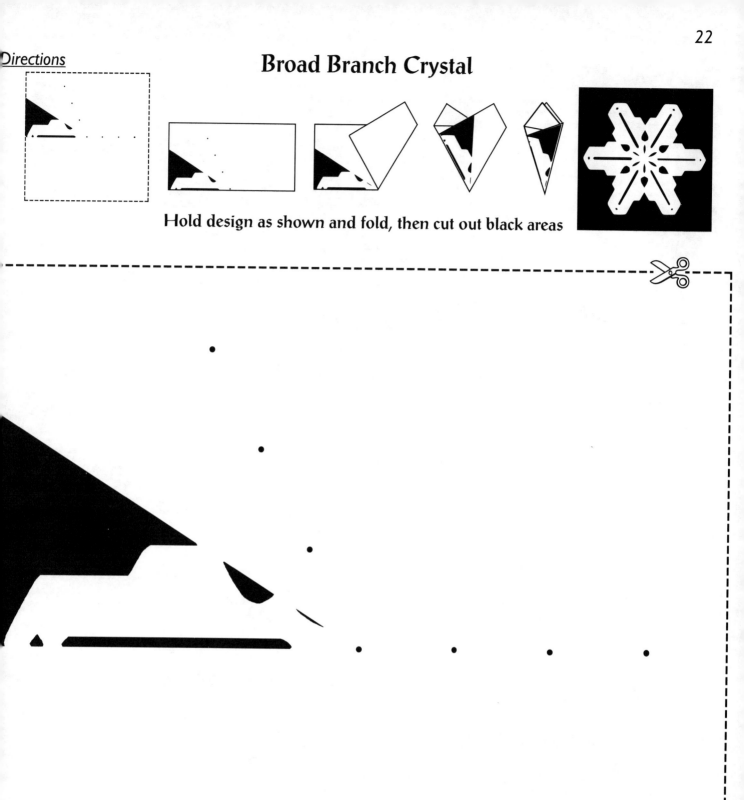

Hold design as shown and fold, then cut out black areas

Dendritic Crystal

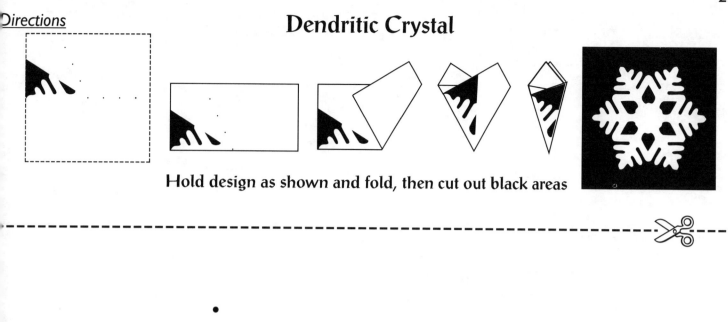

Hold design as shown and fold, then cut out black areas

Crystal Plate

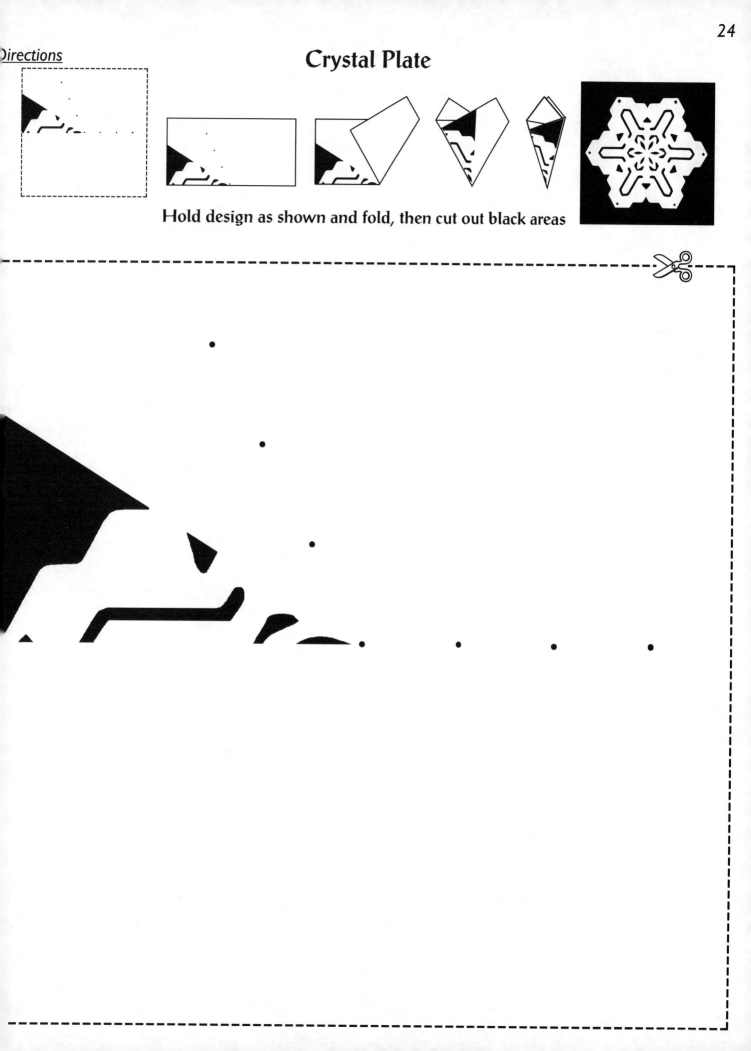

Hold design as shown and fold, then cut out black areas

Snowflakes Are Dancing

Hold design as shown and fold, then cut out black areas

irections

Dendritic Crystal

Hold design as shown and fold, then cut out black areas

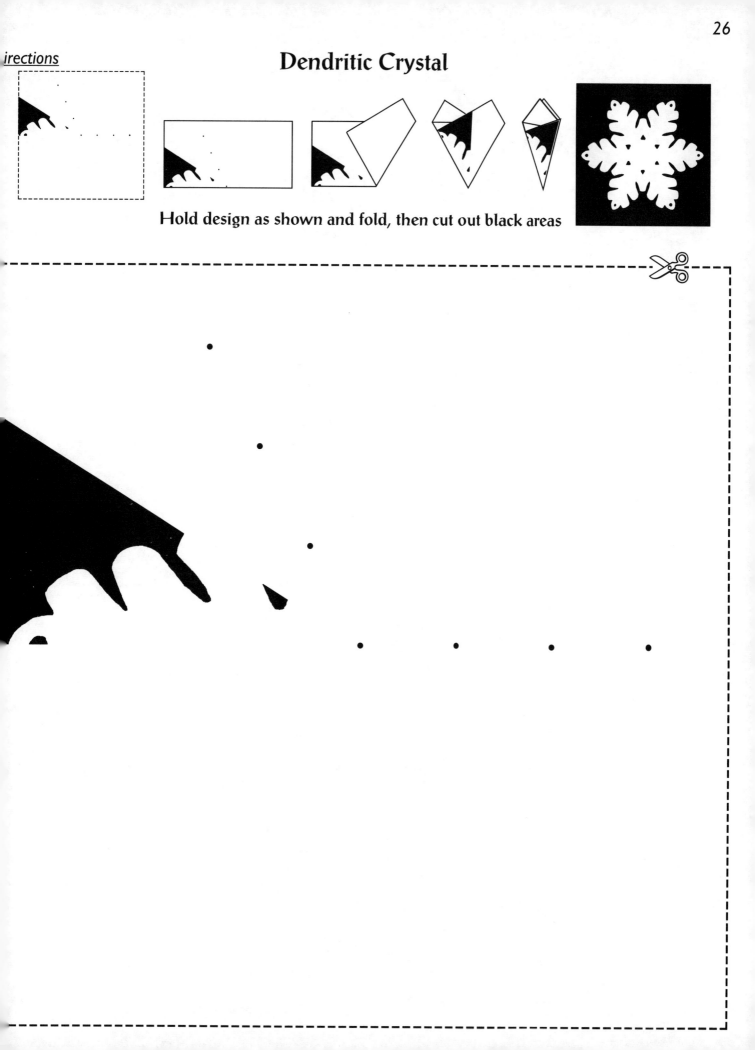

Plate and Sector Branch Crystal

irections

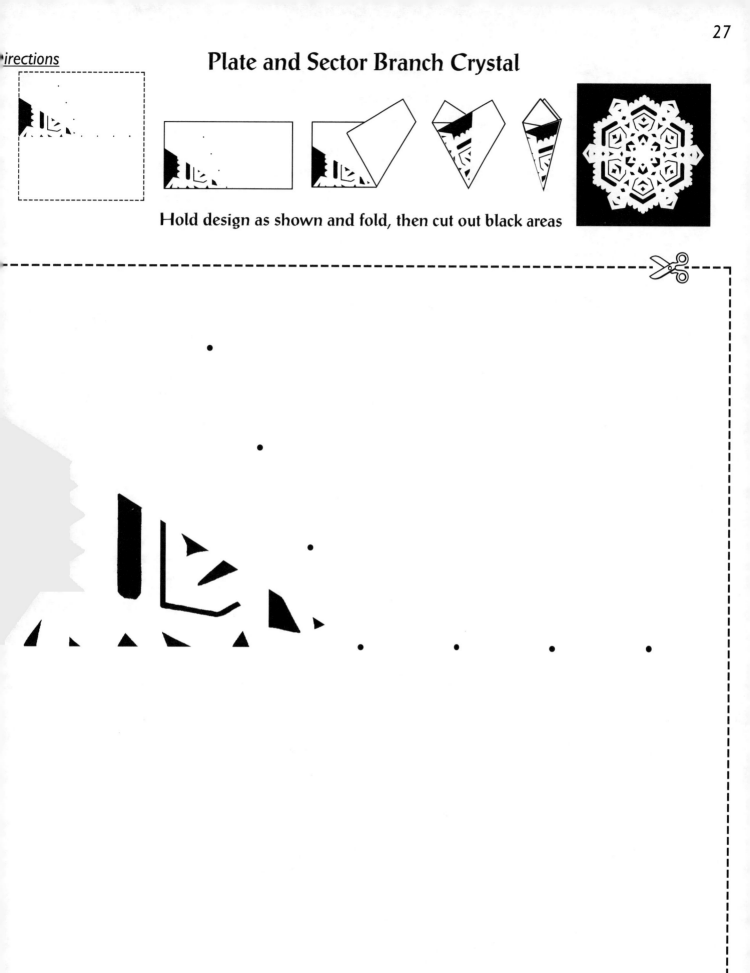

Hold design as shown and fold, then cut out black areas

Dendritic Crystal

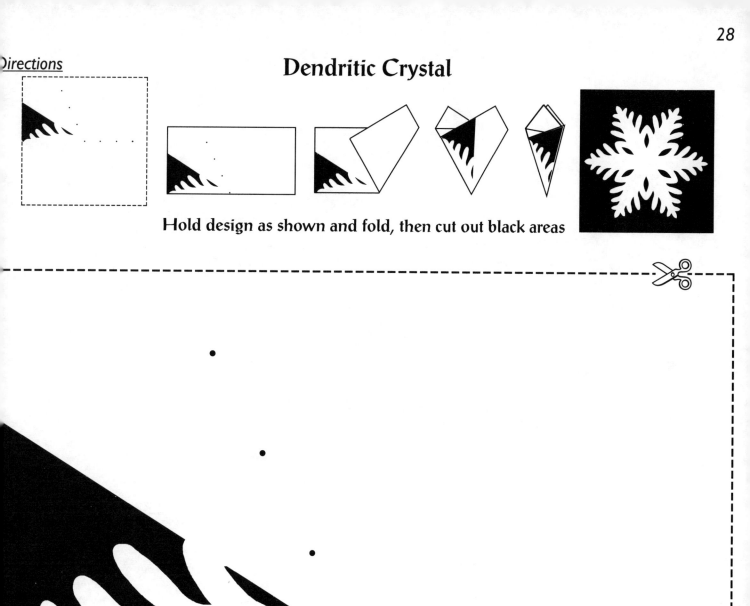

Hold design as shown and fold, then cut out black areas

Dendritic Crystal With Plate Ends

Hold design as shown and fold, then cut out black areas

Snow Blossom

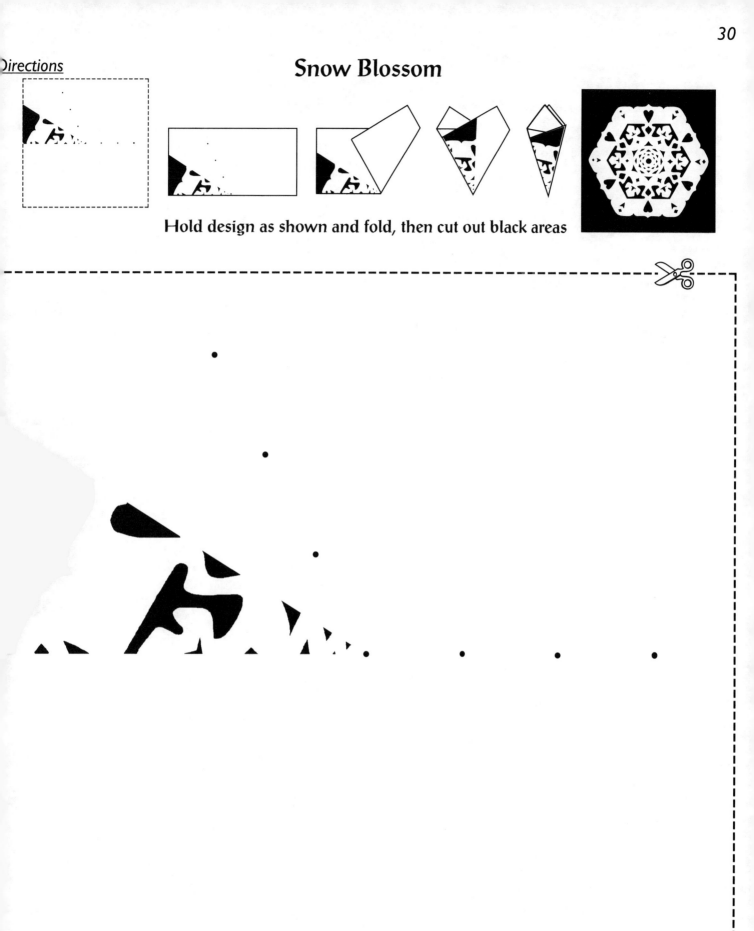

Hold design as shown and fold, then cut out black areas

Dendritic Crystal

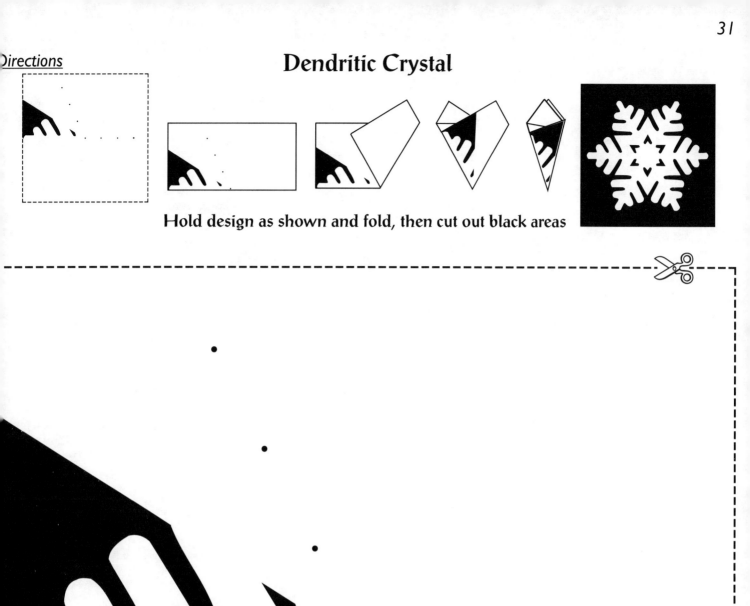

Hold design as shown and fold, then cut out black areas

Hexagram Crystal

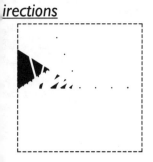

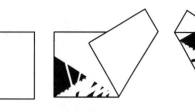 

Hold design as shown and fold, then cut out black areas

Stellar Crystal With Fern-Like Extensions

Hold design as shown and fold, then cut out black areas

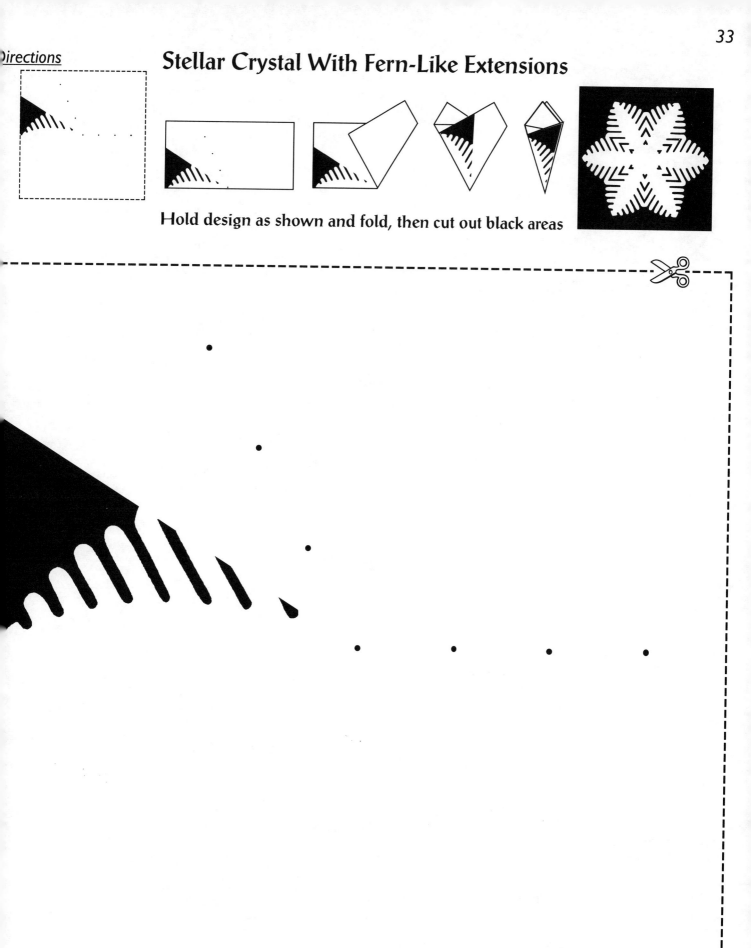

Broad Branch Crystal

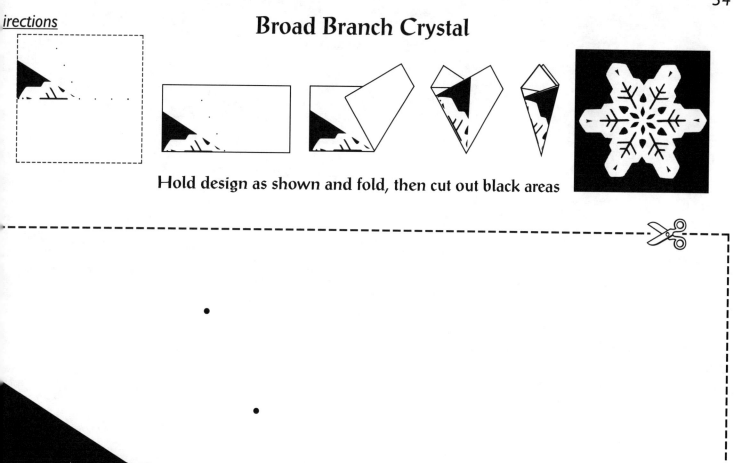

Hold design as shown and fold, then cut out black areas

Dendritic Crystal

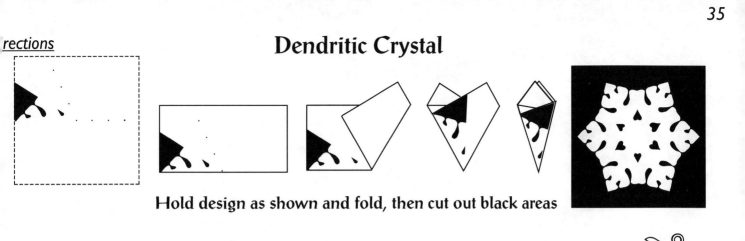

Hold design as shown and fold, then cut out black areas

Dendritic Crystal

Hold design as shown and fold, then cut out black areas

Crystal Star With Simple Extensions

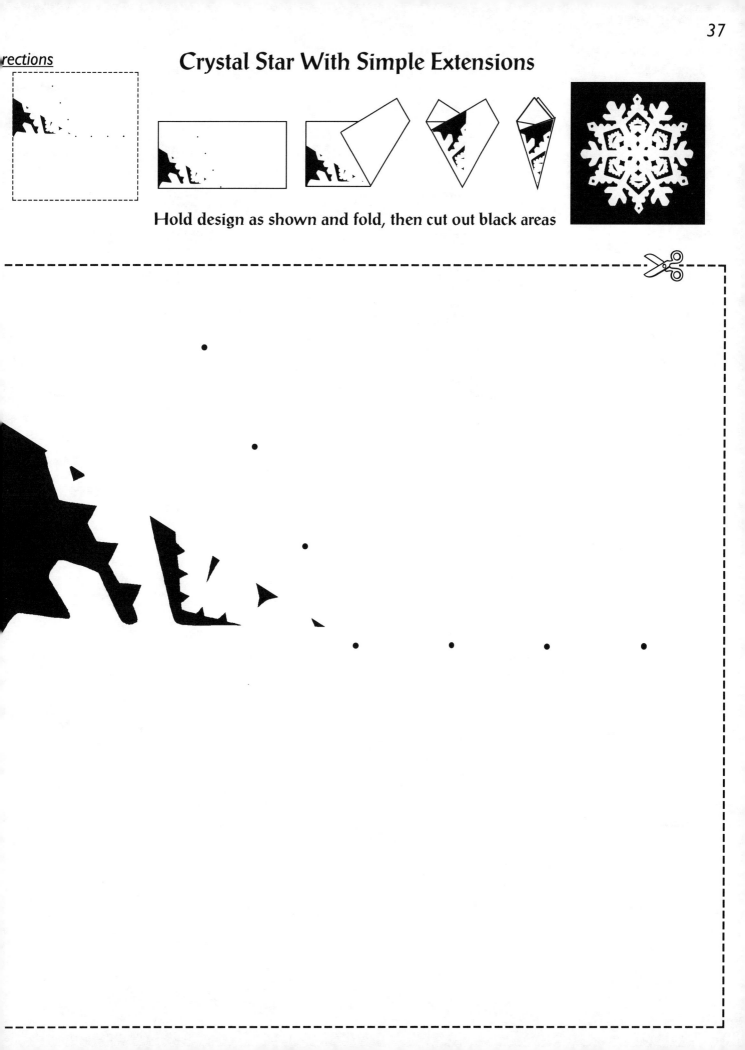

Hold design as shown and fold, then cut out black areas

Sugar Frosted Flake

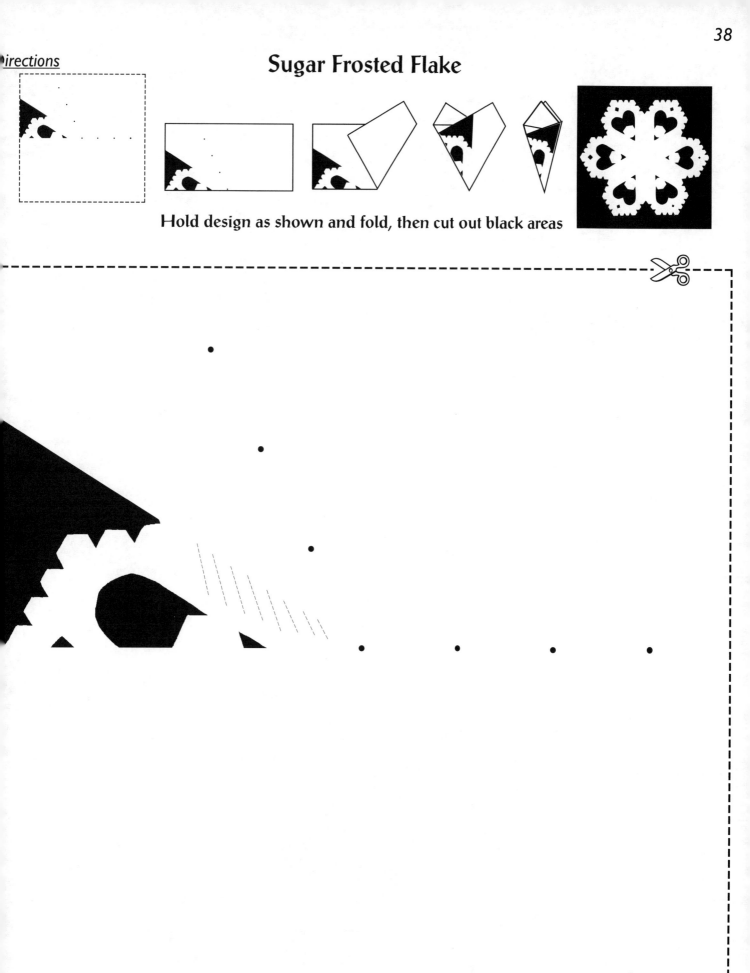

Hold design as shown and fold, then cut out black areas

irections

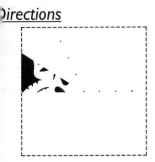

Directions

Valentine Doily

(write a Valentine's message in the center of the finished design)

Hold design as shown and fold, then cut out black areas

Hexagonal Plate Crystal

Hold design as shown and fold, then cut out black areas

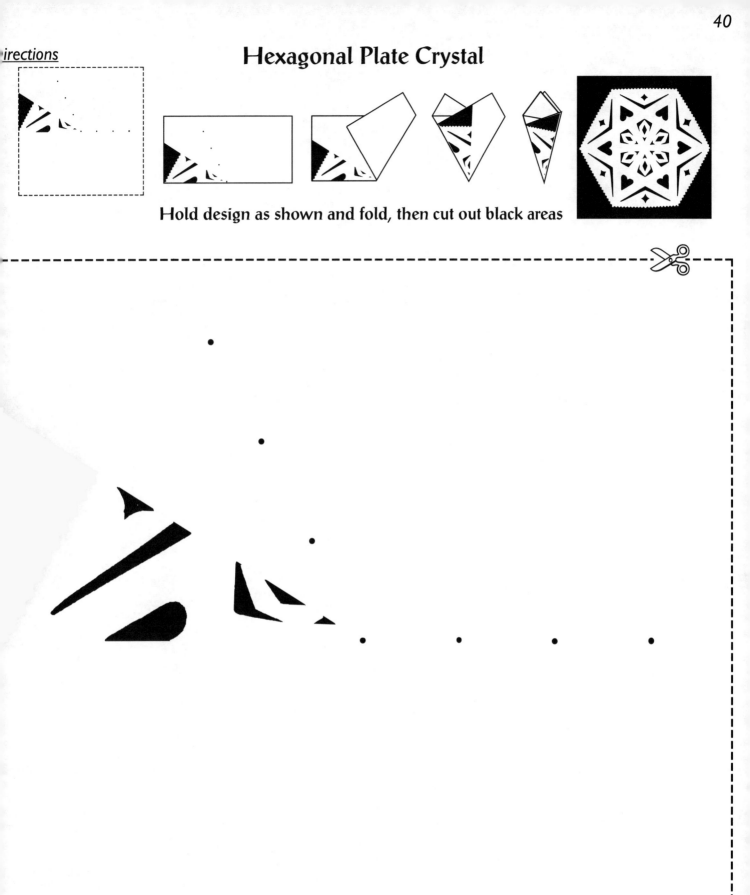

Fern-Like Crystal

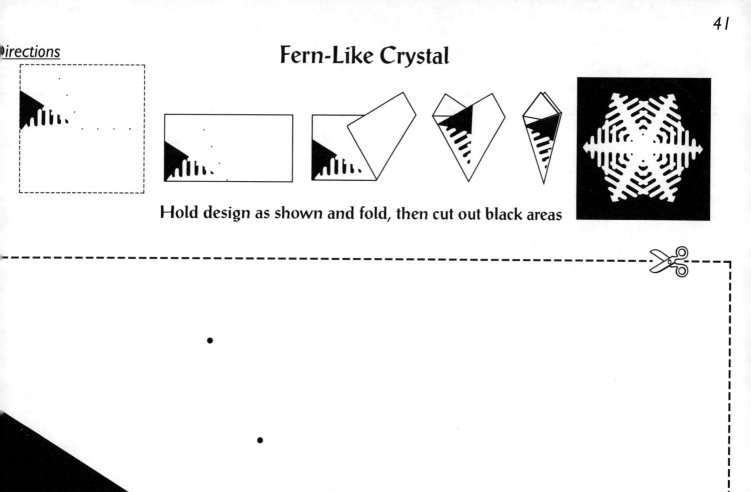

Hold design as shown and fold, then cut out black areas

Crystal Plate With Plate Ends

irections

Hold design as shown and fold, then cut out black areas

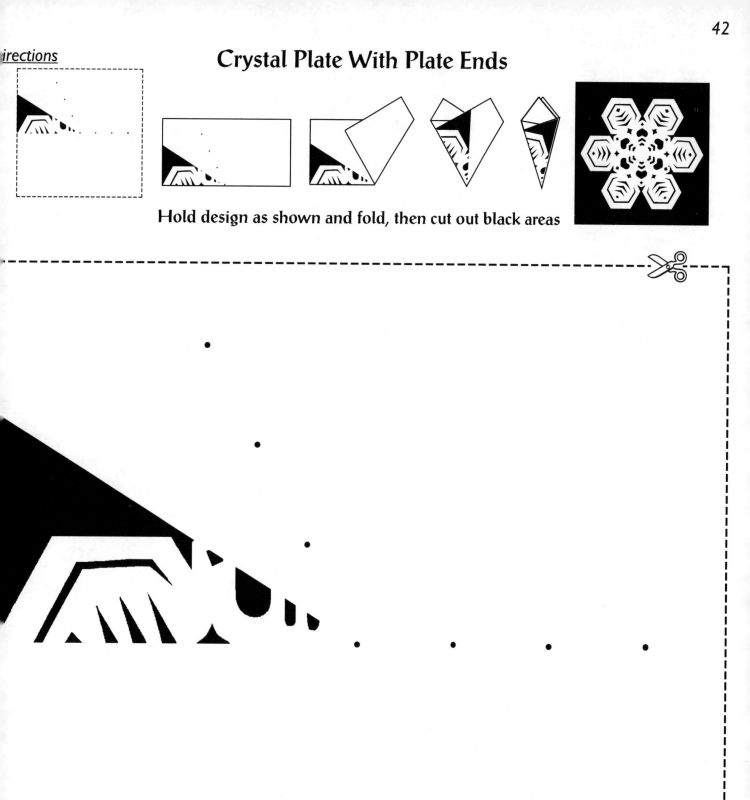

Fern-Like Crystal

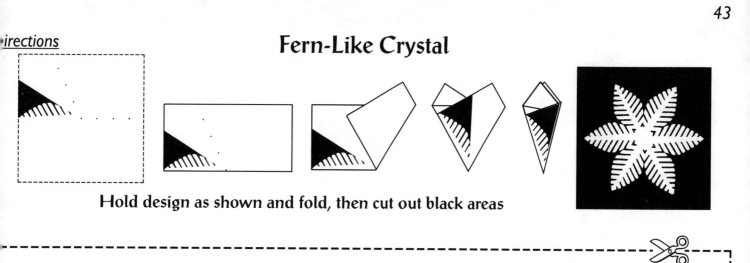

Hold design as shown and fold, then cut out black areas

Crystal Plate With Simple Extensions

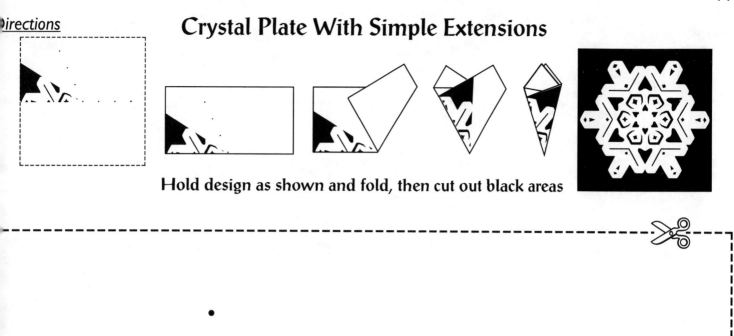

Hold design as shown and fold, then cut out black areas

Star and Broad Branch Crystal

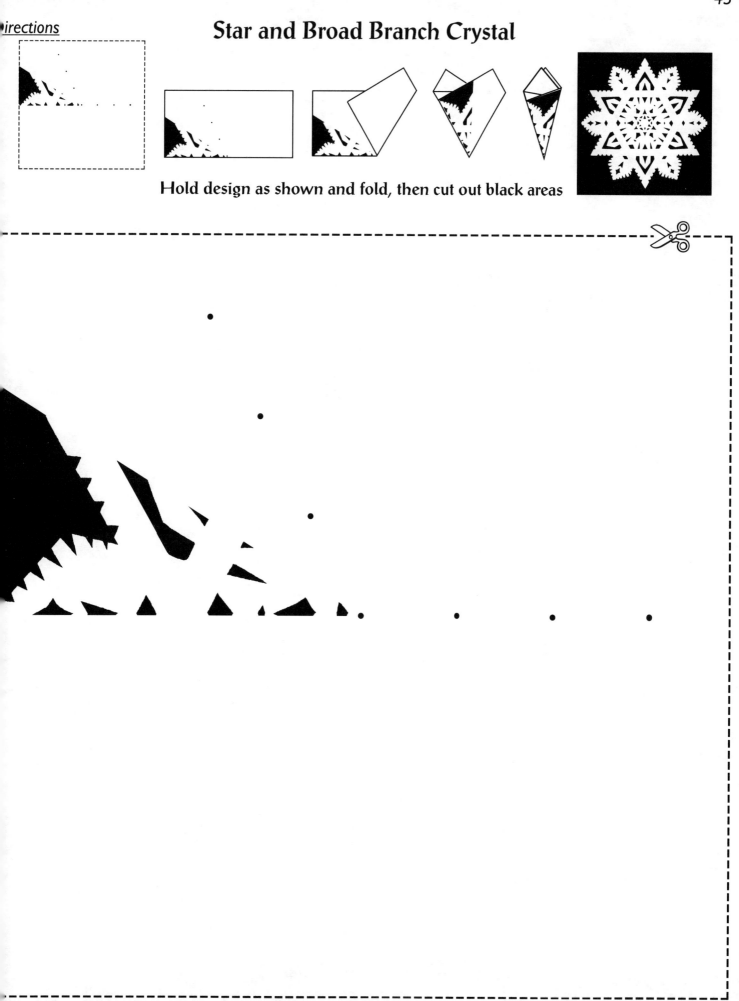

Hold design as shown and fold, then cut out black areas

Snowflake Doily

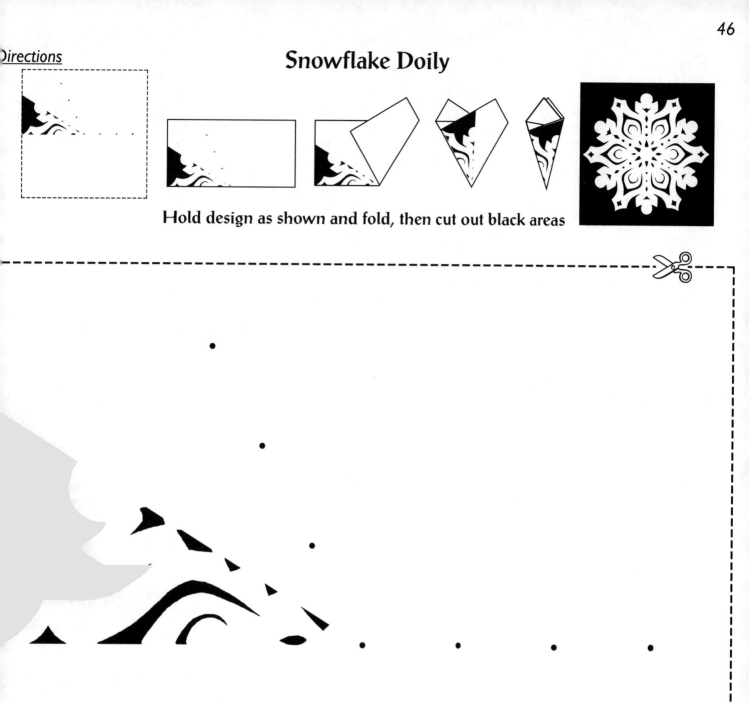

Directions

Hold design as shown and fold, then cut out black areas

47

Snowflake Arizona

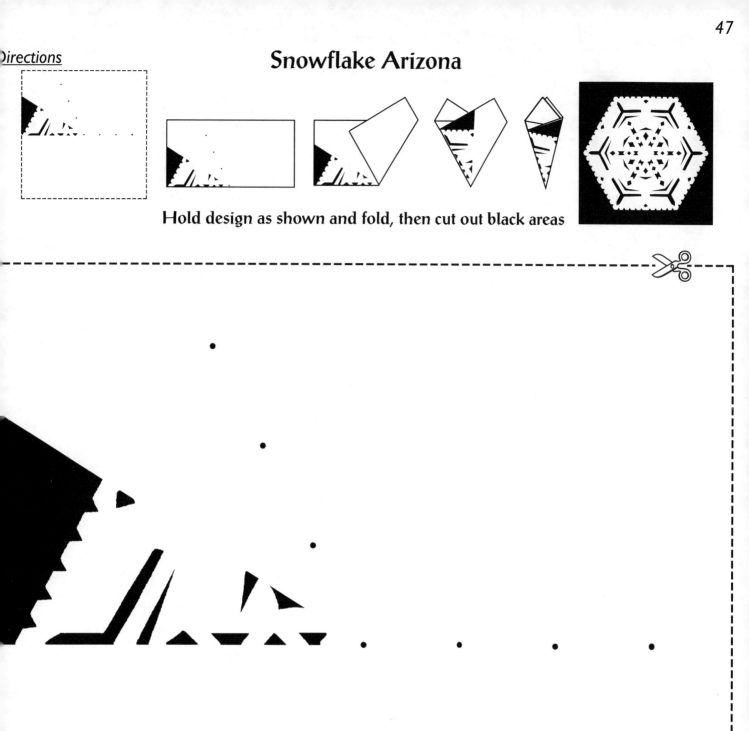

Hold design as shown and fold, then cut out black areas

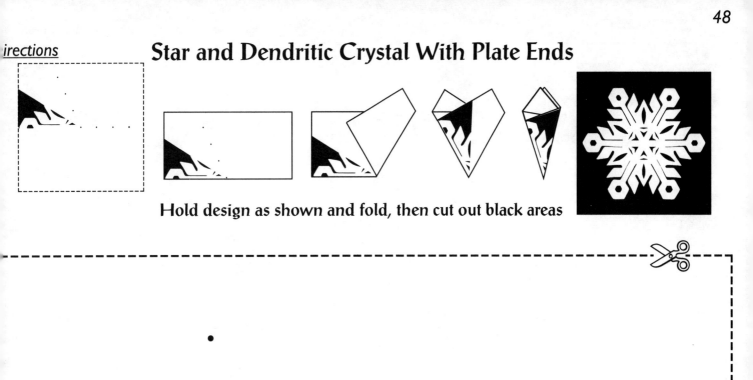

irections

Star and Dendritic Crystal With Plate Ends

Hold design as shown and fold, then cut out black areas

Dendritic Crystal

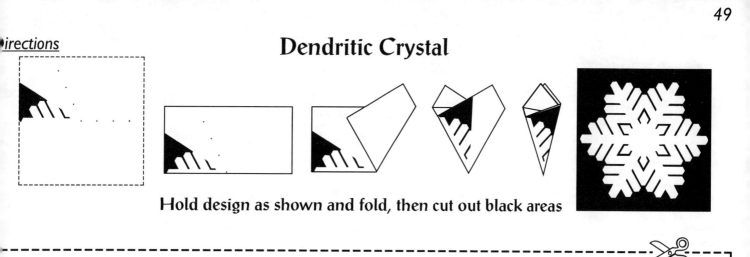

Hold design as shown and fold, then cut out black areas

Crystal Plate With Plate Ends

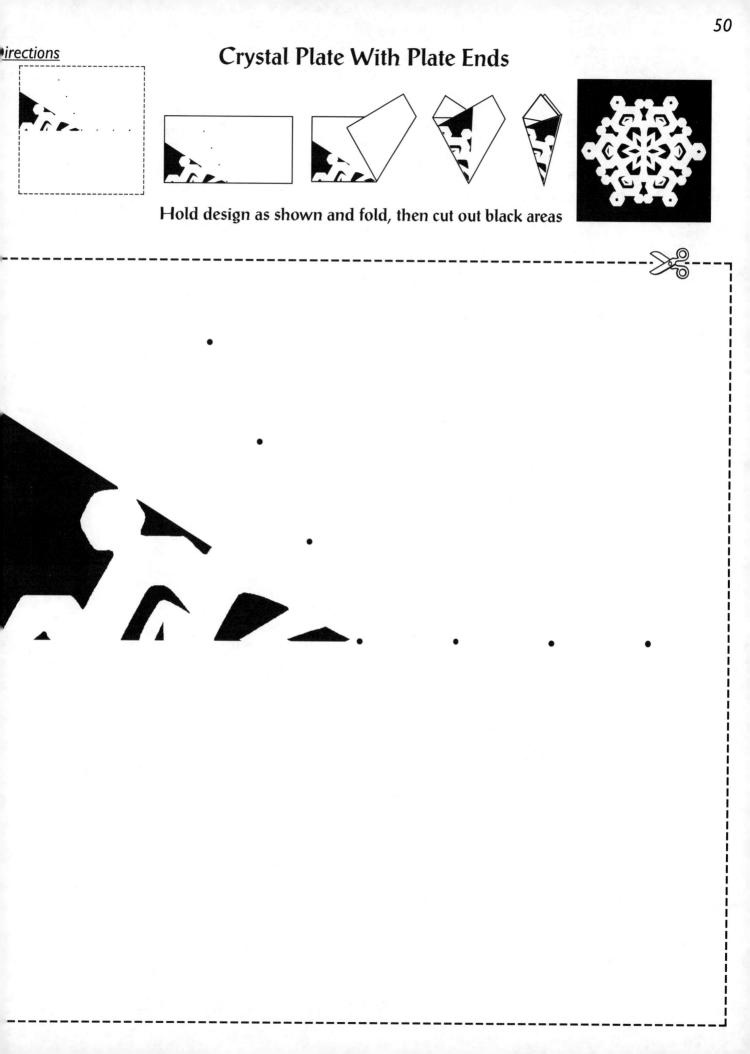

Hold design as shown and fold, then cut out black areas

Fern-Like Crystal

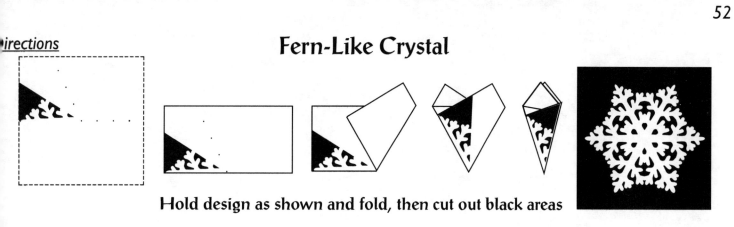

Hold design as shown and fold, then cut out black areas

Crystal Crest

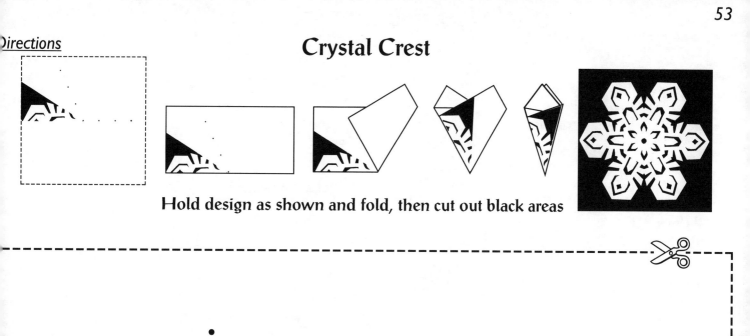

Hold design as shown and fold, then cut out black areas

Broad Branch and Dendritic Crystal

Hold design as shown and fold, then cut out black areas

irections

Twelve Branch Crystal

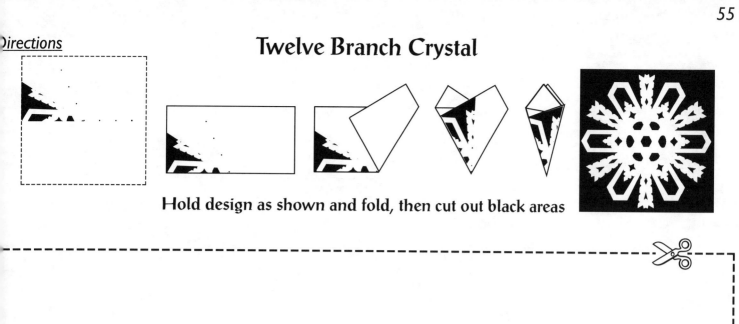

Hold design as shown and fold, then cut out black areas

Aunt Pat's Crystal

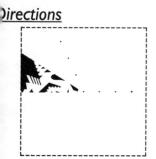   

Hold design as shown and fold, then cut out black areas